My Arctic Adventure at the Top of the World
As a Dew-Liner
September 1969 thru October 1970

Sgt Arthur E Wayland USAF

Cape Lisburne AFS Alaska
711th Aircraft Control and Warning Station

Sergeant Arthur E Wayland
Taken at Cape Lisburne Alaska April 10. 1970

Table of Contents

Preface

This document is about my serving on a military DEWLine radar surveillance site established by the US and Canadian governments to protect both countries during the Cold War between Russia and North America against surprise air attacks on both countries. The Cold war came into beginning after WWII when Joseph Stalin then dictator of Russia fell out of favor with the North American continent countries.

These sites were set up in early 1951 shortly after the end of WWII across the northern arctic border of Canada and the US Territories to give early warning of any air attacks from Russia. Some of these sites were remote to remote isolated. The difference was on a remote site they were located close to some civilization, and on remote isolated sites there were no civilization near by. And absent of female service personnel in fact I know of no women that served on these stations. I was stationed on a remote isolated site on the most western northern end of these sites. These sites stretched from Cape Lisburne on the far western chain all the way to Tule Greenland. To name a few of them, in Alaska there was Lisburne, Liz A, Liz2, Liz3, Point Barrow, Barter Island and on across the arctic circle of Canada it continued approx. 71 sites. These sites were known as the DEWLine (distant early warning line stations). This remote duty's environment by the nature of the terrain was cold and harsh living, some survived and others did not in some way and others just simply went stark crazy mad because of the isolation.

Some of these sites consisted of the Radom coupled with an adjoining support building. Some sites in the mountain terrains were separated with the random located on the mountain and the support buildings known as base camp at the base of the mountain in which case Cape Lisburne fell into this latter category. The mountain Radom was known as top camp and usually consisted of ten or so men. The only access to the top camps was either by a mountain road or by a tramcar system. Cape Lisburne had both of these accesses. An airstrip was near by for rotating men or providing supplies to these camps. Cape Lisburne had an airstrip that ran parallel to the Chukchi Sea (the word has a Russian origin) known as runway 08; and an emergency strip that ran perpendicular to the airstrip 08 known as runway 26. This runway was not authorized, except for emergency take offs. Runway 08 was 4000 feet long. Runway 26 was even shorter and was basically a roadbed that was part of the mountain access road.

These radar sites initially had a range of a few hundred miles and in later years as newer technology was developed had increased ranges. In the late sixties as this technology was developed and implemented some of these sites were deemed obsolete, and were taken out of service where the outer radar bands could cover these obsoleted sites. Cape Lisburne was one of these sites along with the site at Kotzebue that could cover several sites including North East Cape on the Saint Lawrence Island, which was closed in the late 60's.

 In the summer of 1957 "White Alice" communications systems were installed to link these radar sites together and had communication surveillance capabilities. These systems sported big high concrete antennas and usually 60 feet in height and were manned by RCA civilian personnel.

The system initially owned by Federal Electric Company provided the station with communication with all other stations in Alaska for the first time so "White Alice" had it's birth. The Dewline had its beginning and now the American people rest some what easly because the eyes that scan the north can tell the south what is there. Now telephone conversations can be carried on with any telephone exchange within the reach of a Bell system. Teletype messages can be received with the same accuracy with which they were originated.[1]
So, on the 13 of September 1957 "White Alice" at Cape Lisburne went on line.

This was before present day satellite's and was some what in the microwave technology period at this time in history.

When I first arrived there once a month, you could call home for five free minutes and wait for the next month before you could call again. The order in which your turn came up was by DEROS (date of entry received on station) dates. Which simply was the day you arrived in Alaska and not necessarly the day you arrived on site. Then by December these calls were suspended because of flack coming from the wifes of men serving in the south east asia theater. There husband's were not calling enough or did not call so it became a political issue in the government. These free calls on the government meant a lot to the dew-linners because of our isolation from the oposite sex's. It just takes a few to screw up a good thing.

I called home on Christmas day collect and talked to my wife for one hour and it cost us a dollar a minute after the first two minutes. The first two minutes cost two dollars a minute. So, that was my Christmas.

---

[1] *Alaskan Air Command history Elmendorf AFB*

History of Cape Lisburne

I want to give you a little history on Cape Lisburne AFS. The site was originally an Eskimo town by the name of Wevok and existed at this location until 1931. A smallpox epidemic decimated the town and the survivors left the area and only a cemetery remains, which is located on the north side of the present site. This is the only remains of the town and their inhabitants and their presents at this site.

While exploring around one day in the summer of 1970, I came across a pine box with the lid partially exposing a body inside. All of the remains were in the box including the skull. This casket was wedged between some rocks apparently set there because of the permafrost wouldn't allow a hole to be dug. Permafrost line at Cape Lisburne was thirteen feet deep. Apparently from records this gentlemen was a missionary, maybe he was here at the time of the smallpox epidemic. He more than likely passed away during the winter and couldn't be buried.

The sites location is in the northwestern part of Alaska bordered on the west side by the Arctic Ocean and on the northeastern side by the Chuckchi Sea. Cape Liz is within fifty miles of the Russian Coast line. In the map below you can see how close we were from the actual North Pole. This map shows the location circa 1953. Cape Liz is Located at Lat. 68-52-30-46N;Longitude 166-6-39.895W. Airport designation LUR, radio call sign "PALU" .

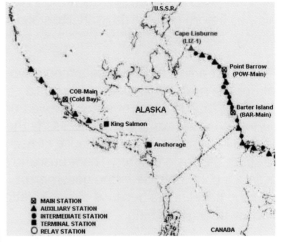

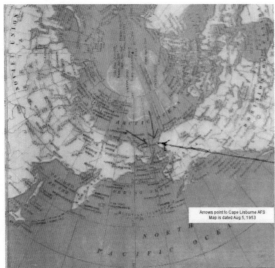

Arrows point to Cape Lisburne AFS
Map is dated Aug 5, 1953

According to the Air Force on September 8, 1974, the only reported incident of UFO's at Cape Lisburne occurred. There is no further mention of the following account, so the official explanation. If any, is unknown.

" A little before 0400. A steady point of light was observed passing rapidly at what appeared to be high altitude over our station. From horizon to horizon in the next couple of hours seven more such objects were seen passing overhead in an east-west track and one from north to south: five traveling in formation. None of these registered on the Operations radarscopes. Coordination with ANRCC and Murphy Dome, Kotzebue and Liz 2 yielded no explanation. Five or six people, including the Operations officer, observed this phenomenon. " [2]

In the fall of 1976, AAC (Alaskan Air Command) requested bids from civilian companies to assume operations and maintenance of all functions at the site, except radar operations and postal service. This idea had been proposed twenty years earlier.

In 1983 Cape Lisburne was converted to a satellite-monitored site with one dish located at where base camp used to reside. All military personnel were reassigned to other places.

Satellite imagining reveals just a butler style steel building next to this Satellite antenna. I cannot imagine how it is powered. All of the new facilities that were there in 1970 are gone. In searching the Internet I found documents where they returned the site back to its original environment. Cleaned up all traces of the PCB's left in the earth by fuel oil etc. Most of the original buildings have been removed.

---

[2] From the radarmuseum.com/cape Lisburne/documents/commanders report

ATT Alascom Earth Station at Cape Lisburne, Alaska
November 10, 1998

Even though it has been forty-eight years since I was there serving my country, it seems such a waste of material and manpower. The expense the government went to in improving the facilities for future airmen to serve at this site. However since President Ronald Regan's request in his speech while visiting the Berlin wall to "tear that wall down" was the end of the cold war era warriors that served on these stations.

I dedicate this document to my Granddaughter Bonnie Rose for making my YouTube video and inspiring me to make it and I also dedicate it to Leslie Randal of Orem Utah the granddaughter of Hugh and Elnor Yancey the USO entertainer's who lost there lives at Cape Lisburne on July 16,1966 in an airplane crash who found my video's and contacted me to help in her research of this tragic crash. This site is her grandparent's final resting place. She inspired me to write this document depicting the life of a "dew-Liner."

Now, on to experiencing my Arctic adventure. I had already served three years in the United States Air Force when given this assignment. I was called up due to the urgency of the Vietnam War escalation. I had taken my basic training at Amarillo, TX in the fall of 1966. I was stationed at the following bases: 1360th Civil Engineers at Orlando AFB Florida for eighteen months and the 436th MAW at Dover AFB Delaware for thirteen months serving with the 436th Civil Engineers, when I received orders to serve with the Alaskan Air Command assigned to North East Cape, Saint Lawrence Island Alaska. This was a Norad radar station located in the Baltic Ocean between Alaska and Russia. I had only been married two years when I received this assignment, so it was going to be hard on the both of us to be separated because this site was remote isolated duty.

I had recently been promoted in July of 1969 to the rank of E-4 (newly named sergeant). I was trained in the USAF as a heating systems specialist (in lay men's terms a Boiler operator) Having taken a thirty day leave I left my wife for parts unknown to me and of course without her. We parted our ways at the air terminal and I was off to Alaska for a one-year tour of duty after which we had decided that I would not reenlist. Having a stop over at McCord Air Force Base in Tacoma Washington and after spending the night there, I departed for Elmendorf AFB at Anchorage Alaska with a week of survival school. After all I was going where some dangerous conditions and wildlife existed. Upon my arrival at Elmendorf and reporting to the assignment section to turn my orders in I was informed that my orders had been changed, I was being reassigned to a different radar station, because the year before some radar stations had been up graded with their equipment and the ranges were greater, so some had been closed. North East Cape, on Saint Lawrence Island being one of them, so hence I was going to the 711th AC&W radar site at Cape Lisburne. I had no clue as to where this station was located geographically. In the evening while taking my evening meal at the transient barracks I looked on a topography relief map mounted on a wall looking for the location of my new assignment. When I located it at the top of the world I sure was surprised, its location was 570 miles Northwest of Fairbanks. I now had to study the survival of dealing with the wolverine, Grizzly, and the Polar bear plus the harsh weather in which I was going to in counter. This was definitely going to be an interesting tour of duty.

Having spent the week completing survival school, and procuring my fifty pounds of cold weather gear and checked out medically at Elmendorf AFB, I was off. I was notified around four in the evening to pack everything up. I was leaving the transient barracks for Nome, then to Kotzebue and evidentially the Cape. We departed Elmendorf and headed for Nome. The day was about over and the sun was setting over Alaska, but at 40,000 feet we could see the curvature of the earth with snow covered terrain and over Russia it was still sunny. It was a beautiful flight with the snow glistening on the earth's surface as the planes shadow passed over the snow. We crossed the Arctic Circle on this night, which was October 2, 1969, landing at Nome to let departing passenger's leave the plane. Two stewardesses and I departed for Kotzebue for the final destination of this flight of which I was the only passenger. The plane refueled and returned to Anchorage by 0600. We arrived after six hours from Elmendorf; it was midnight by Alaskan standard time. Someone from the Eskimo village took me to the Kotzebue air station, which sat upon a knawel; there I spent the night in a bed in the hallway. Some accommodations, the weather was very foggy that night. Their chow hall was closed for the night and it was a good thing I had a snack earlier. I was abruptly awakened by a horn that sounded like we were in a submarine and the order had been given to dive. This turned out to be a Klaxon horn of which I would eventually get used to. It was no drill-Russian TU_95 Bears (aircraft that looked like B-52 bombers) were among us. Being a temporary guest, a fellow airman told me to follow him, so we wound up in their motor pool. Still no breakfast for that morning, guess I was adapted to being a seven day camel. Later that morning I was taken back to the airfield for my departure to Cape Lisburne. By 10:00 am the fog still had not lifted, the little Piper Cub type aircraft they called a bush plane operated by Wein airlines was on standby and being loaded with food and short supplies, as they liked to call them. Since I was the only passenger going

to Lisburne they asked if I wanted to go on that flight when the fog lifted or wait until later in the day. If I went then they would have to leave my baggage and cold weather gear there because they had reached there load limit with my weight included. I opted to go then rather than go back to the radar station at Kotzebue. At least I would get there for noon chow. This was the worst mistake I could have made not haven been in Alaska before. The temp at Lisburne was a balmy -20 below when I arrived. I had to stay in the confines of the site buildings to stay warm. The plane later came in that afternoon with my gear. I immediately dug in to the cold weather bag and found the parka and put it on. The moral of this situation is to never leave things to chance because it will come back to bite you. If the plane had not been able to land for several days I would have been screwed.

After donning my parka, I was given a tour of the site from a Staff Sargent from Memphis Tennessee. I do not recall his name but he was assigned to the boiler room. I

remember I always had to ask him to repeat what he was saying, because he would always turn his head away from me while he talked, so finally I had enough of that and asked him to repeat his self because I could not hear or understand what he was saying. He was due to rotate back to the states for his years tour was about up, so I guess the year made him shy as I was about to experience a similar loneliness and desire not to talk too much. The Air Force painted this to be a lovely site with winters harsh and to keep the tours to a maximum of one year for physiological reasons. Just a note, we had two people to go crazy the year I was there and for good reason.

Looking back it is a wonder I didn't because you can be around eighty-five men and still be lonely. This site was a remote isolated place and no women were allowed there. We were in the land of the midnight sun, which consisted of twenty-four hours of daylight in the late spring thru the summer until September. In late October the sunlight disappeared and we had twenty-three hours of total darkness. The other half an hour

 was a gray dusky light that one experiences just before it gets dark. This last until around mid February and as you can see some of the curvature of the earth that far north the sun rotates around the horizon in about 270 degree arch and eventually rise to straight overhead in July. In the winter temps get as low as -90 and as high as +72 degrees F in the summer. One night we had a one hundred mile an

hour wind that took the chill factor to -135 degrees. I experienced many of a night viewing the aura borealis (northern lights), which is a beautiful site to see. Weather can change at a moments notice and stay that way for days with the winds picking up to make it impossible for planes to land on the 4000-foot runway. We once went for eighteen days without any contact from the outside world. We had no Television, Radio (except for armed forces radio, and reception was poor at the least and was controlled by the communication section) cell service, which was not practical in those days and was non-existent, nor any newspapers except one that was brought in via some troop arriving for his tour of duty. You did receive mail when the Wein pilot came in from Kotzebue, about the only thing to keep you sane was to keep busy with your main job or have an auxiliary jobs such as working in the laundry washing and pressing other airmen's clothes, barbering if you knew how since we did not have a Barber shop, working in the NCO club bar tendering, sweeping and cleaning floors for the construction personnel and keeping their quarters clean, and a non paying job of ordering flowers for special occasions thru a florist shop in Anchorage which was passed on as you rotated out, or talk which you soon run out of things to talk about. We did have a rec hall that consisted of several pool tables, several card tables a fosse ball table a small library of outdated books from the fifties, a craft shop/store where you could make anything from ceramics to anything leather [I made my wife a leather pocket book], and a small movie theater. When the film arrived there were some current flicks that was being shown in the states. We had an emergency pack of movies to be used when we were severally snowed in.

We had a medic assigned to Lisburne for general health care and first aide anything else you were medevac to Anchorage to Fort Richardson [I had a tooth to go dead and turned black as coal but did not warrant being sent there for treatment]. We were eight hundred and fifty six miles from Anchorage. There were Chaplin's of all dominations that rotated in and out during the year and usually stayed a day or so depending on the weather; sometimes we had services on Sunday (when they were there) other times they just talked to us to see if we had any problems. As far as refreshment's we had cokes with no fizz and candy bars that had turned white due to there being cold. Some how sugar causes the chocolate to turn white when cold.

I experienced a lot of strange phenomena's while there, one was seeing the moisture in the wood of a door come thru it and ice cycles forming on the inside of the boiler room from an outside door and were laced horizontally from the 100 mph wind blowing-

outside. I have seen wolverine, grizzlies, polar bear, arctic foxes, and wolves that kept howling all night. I even saw Sargent Preston of the Yukon one night (an old radio show in the late 40's). Coming out of the boiler plant one night going to mid night chow there was a dog sled team all hitched up and the dogs laying down resting. A Canadian Royal mounted police officer in the chow hall stopping for rest until he could complete his journey north. He was in pursuit of a fugitive that had killed an Eskimo while on a hunting party apparently caught his Eskimo wife in bed with another Eskimo male. I have experienced white outs, where it's snowing so hard that you can't see your hand in front of your face, there is no direction in as far as determining whether you are going left or right or back from where you came. We had ropes tied between doorways to place your hand on to lead you to the next doorway (if one choose not to use these ropes you would get lost and may freeze to death). The site was being renovating due to an upgrade of the site and a composite building being built and a lot of the inter hall ways had been removed. Construction had begun in 1968 and was completed the summer of 1970.

How Am I Going To Got to work [3]

---

[3] Picture taken from M.Sgt. Gary Johnson's tour in 1966 by permission

The Cape was definitely a lonely place wolves were very prevalent at night and almost weird as you heard their howls looking for food of prey or just calling for their mates. I don't believe they would hurt you if left alone. I once saw one and it seemed to not want any contact with a human. The Ptarmigan (the Alaska state bird) were everywhere during the summer months. Caribou seemed to me to be the dumbest animal. They would follow paths on the road and seemed to fear no one. Seals would lie on the frozen sea pack just sunning them selves. The Chukchi Sea was our shoreline and in the rocks west of the site a bird known as a Muir nested in these rocks and hatched their young. There was an abundance of wild life such as the Grizzly bear, now this bear is dangerous when confronted. In the spring of 1970 while transferring water to top camp I encountered one that had wondered into the bowels of the tram shack's machinery room. We had a transfer accumulation tank located in this room and pumps to transfer the water up 2000 feet to top camp. As I descended the stairs from the trams ground level to approach this tank, I was startled to see him or her not knowing how to tell gender. The bear immediately rose to about 8 feet on its haunches when I was seen, so I eased back up the stairs and returned the next morning and it was gone. We had no weapons except the standard M-1 carbine, which was always locked, in the communication room at camp. These weapons were only for defensive encounters with the enemy and drills. Some of the civilians working for the White Alice station had their

own hunting weapons with permits to have them.

We were only 50 miles from the Russian coast and could be seen on a very clear day from Top Camp as seen in this picture. The Russians had an espionage-training center another fifty miles inland, so besides our mission of air surveillance was to monitor their radio traffic chatter. We encountered many flyovers by them and their trying to listen with their sophisticated electronic equipment to us. They were aware of everyone's names that arrived and departed. These planes were similar to our B-52 bombers and were known as a Russian Bear aircraft. When they would get near we were alerted during the day and night time via the infamous klaxon horn that I mentioned earlier and we would man our battle stations. The USAF fighter squadron of F-105's was scrambled from their bases in the center of Alaska and somewhere in Canada. This was known as the cold war of the 1950's and 60's. We were the most outer western edge of the DEW line system established across the arctic after WWII. So, you see anyone that served in the Military at the top of the World was known as a "dew-liner". Some on the DEW Line in the center, duty was not so bad except for small auxiliary stations consisting of 10-to 15 men, but the Cape was harsh living at most. As I mentioned earlier, being that far north (168 miles from Kotzebue and 286 miles above the Arctic circle and the closest civilization an Eskimo village known as Point Hope 25 miles away) besides the weather we experienced days of constant daylight or darkness depending upon the season of the year. During the days of total darkness planes landing at Lisburne had firepots that lined each side of the runway as they approached and if you weren't busy and could be spared you helped set these firepots out. After the Aircraft departed these firepots were extinguished and removed.

Thanksgiving and Christmas day of 1969 was celebrated and a nice noon meal with a bottle of cold duck (wine) and Turkey with all of the trimmings were served. We had an outstanding baker that made all of our pastries, cakes, and pies. He had made the Air Force a career and been in Alaska for several years serving at various sites. We were just lucky he was with us that year. If you were of the rank E-4 and below you were expected to pull KP duty in the mess hall twice during your tour by yourself. On one of my KP times I was handling dishes so fast to place in the clipper that I broke a dish on the sink and a piece embedded into my hand and I still wear that piece today as a souvenir.

In the chow hall hung a polar bear hide with head and claws and was given to the site in 1968. This hide hung on a back wall for all to see including visitors and I am sure for first time visitors it was a shock to see (as seen in this picture of me having a cup of coffee). While I was there a team of people from the University of Oregon came to tag these bears with electronic tracking devices embedded under their skin in order to track their movements across the ice pack. A fixed wing aircraft and a helicopter arrived to preform this function. These people were pilots and several Veterinarians to tranquilize the bears with a dart shot from the helicopter to immobilize the bears in order to insert these devices. The site commander told us that any non-essential personnel were invited to ride out on the ice pack to observe them. Unfortunately I was not able to go, but paid someone for pictures to be taken on a Polaroid camera. These pictures were lost in the 1980's unfortunately.

We had a small PX (post-exchange) where you could buy small items when they had them. I had my wife to send soap, toothpaste, and tooth brush every three months because they were in short supply of those items. Writing supplies were available except ballpoint pens, so I had my wife to send me those as well.

We had a small post office manned by a trained US mail service airmen; there were small pigeon holed mailboxes with individual locks. He handled anything from letters to packages. He handled the mail in secure pouches to and from the bush plane. I wrote my wife a letter ever day that consisted of twenty or thirty pages per day for three hundred eighty days. I served over four years in the military because I had less than a year to go when I received this assignment.

I became friends with our weatherman and he taught me a lot about the weather in recognizing cloud formations and what to expect out of them. Every morning at precisely 0900 he listened to a Morse code signal from Elmendorf and when the code for LUR (.-.., ..-, .-.) came up he had to report the weather at Lisburne. This information was relayed to all airports for their daily flight plans. Then he had these weather radio beacon's and sent one a loft each day to gather weather and barometric pressures at different altitudes.

Snow depths were eight feet or higher and drifts could easily reach thirty feet in places. Our water supply came from the trickling of water buried under the snow in a special ravine north of the site in which was called a water gallery with a vertically placed steel culvert of approx. three feet in diameter and forty feet deep with a trap door about a third of the way down for viewing how much water was accumulated and sometimes in the spring the trap door was

not visible because of high water levels. In the winter you had to drop down into this culvert in order to have access to the trap door. In this pipe at the bottom existed a submergible pump in which we were able to pump water into several accumulation tanks.

We had several track masters and two snowmobiles; these vehicles were for use in an emergency. They were started once a week in order to keep them operational, one of them could hold eight men and the other one was a small one that had a four-man occupancy. They were housed in a building for protection from the elements and I remember one was red and the other one was blue with the standard US Air Force markings on them. We used the snowmobiles for fun occasionally, I remember driving one and was amazed how fast they would travel. On our off time when the weather had cleared we made our own recreation by doing snowball fights like we used to at home when we were kids, but we had to be extremely careful not to damage government property because we were considered government property.

We would hike to top camp, which was a five-mile trek by the access road from base camp. This gave us good exercise. I was used to hiking as a younger man since I was a teenager. I belonged to the Boy Scouts and hiked over 200 miles in the Great Smokey Mountains where I was born and raised. I tried to keep myself in shape while at Cape Lisburne. I lost sixty-five pounds while there and weighed 165 pounds when discharged from the Air Force. Upon returning home in the fall of 1970, my wife commented that my neck was so long I looked like Ichabod Crane.

Encounter with Russian Spy Ship

One evening, in late spring after the Chukchi Sea had thawed, I was returning to duty and coming from the Rec halls outer door which put me on an access road which was a short way back to the steam plant I looked toward the beach and about 100 yards off shore were two Russian trawlers just sitting there. I could see the sailors on board looking at me and I of course could see their activity. I could not believe my eyes, for I had seen in books the famous half moon and cycle and there it was in living color and real life. Their radar antennas were rotating as if they were picking up signals from us. Upon returning to the boiler room office, I notified the commander by phone. He told me he was aware of the situation and to please hang up because they were listening to our conversations. The weather conditions that evening were clear until the fog rolled in later during dusk. I looked again at the shoreline and the Russian ships had left through the fog never to be seen again. I now know their mission was to spy on our newly constructed facility and some of the new electronic gear we had installed. This equipment had not completely gone "HOT" which was not to be until later. Also, after this, Japan had a Tsunami and within weeks Japanese glass

fishing balls were showing up on the edge of the beach, which were rather festive.

In March, the fuel barge out of San Francisco, Calf. that left in January working it's way North delivered our No 2 Arctic fuel for the next winter, which both the steam plant and generator plant used. I participated in the operation of refueling our two 220,000 gallon tanks.

In June, operation "Cool Barge" arrived from California with Groceries and staples, equipment parts, beer, meat, etc. Everyone participated in this operation that could be spared for eighteen hours. The barges (ten in all) arrived around 0300 and while they were prepping to come ashore, we had breakfast and job assignments were handed out. Around 0500 the operation began by LST's coming ashore with trucks and equipment to transfer various items around the site quickly. All through the day trucks were shuttling back and forth between these landing craft and the main barges. It almost looked like pictures of D-day in WWII. There were sailors directing traffic depending on the color of the vehicle, which designated what each was carrying. This turned out to be the longest day and at the end of it we were all exhausted. Our duties were to unload the pallets

and organize the items had to rock us to sleep turned around and we were their last stop radar station on the went back to normal the were for the airmen that for the next year of 1970

brought to shore. No one that night. The ships headed south because and the most Northern DEW-line system. Things next day. These supplies were to be assigned here to 1971.

In the summer of 1970 we had equipment that needed to return to Elmendorf because by then all construction had about ceased and was still winding down in some areas. A C-124 (known as the flying Pig) out of Elmendorf arrived to pick this equipment up. In the process of landing the plane a USAF reservist pilot out of the lower forty-eight while descending to a lower altitude and having put the plane in a steeper glide path; blew one of the outboard engines but was able to safely land. So, for the next week and new parts arrived by Wein Airlines, a former aircraft mechanic that had crossed trained into the motor pool was allowed to make repairs to the engine. The manifold was cracked and required welding which was done in addition to adding the broken part. After a week the plane was ready to be loaded with this equipment. I had befriended a radio repairman out of Anchorage several months before and he was in and out of the Cape. He took that flight back to Elmendorf that day; one of the pieces of equipment that was loaded was a huge ditch digger weighing about 6,000 pounds. The next month the radio repairman was back, so I asked him if the flight back went ok. He told me somewhere southeast of the cape the C-124 started to lose altitude, so the pilot ordered the back doors opened and he put the plane in an upward stall and all of that equipment was released as he witnessed it hit the ground with a splatter. They were able to limp to Galina AFS and land the plane. Galina was like Kotzebue and had an airstrip that would accommodate bigger aircraft, so he returned on a C-130 to Anchorage.

Aircraft accidents occurred every now and then in Alaska, I have a short story to tell, One day while at Top Camp in the early spring the water was unusually blue and crystal clear which indicates very cold water temperatures I spotted what appeared to be the tail of an aircraft about fifty or so feet below the surface partially resting on a ledge. I inquired if any one knew what happened I was told lore had it that it crashed in 1966 and that there were bodies still in it. I was taught in survival school that at those temperatures that a body will freeze to death in less than three minutes. Like taking your breath away from the cold and then you are gone. When I returned to base camp and looking into some steam plant logs of that year I found the description that someone was nice enough to log. The accident occurred on July 16, 1966 and a USO show was on it and the aircraft type was a C-123. Recently several years ago I along with my granddaughters help created a YouTube video of Cape Lisburne. This year the youngest Granddaughter of the USO people contacted me and these were her Grand parents. I won't get into details here for she has created a web site devoted to them named *PaintYourBluesAway.com*, which you can follow. Her grand parents were Hugh and Elnor Yancey, he was an artist like the late Bob Ross and could paint an oil coloring in less than a minute. They traveled to military bases in Alaska and South East Asia entertaining troops.

Another accident occurred at Cape Lisburne on January 26, 1963. A C-46F-1CU Commando carrying mail met its fate in a similar way on its approach to the airstrip. Its remains are located only 100 yards away from the 1966 accident. The pilot survived and the co-pilot drowned. After this accident mail was delivered by Wein airlines Company.

Tragedy's occurred now and then, we had an airmen to die while I was there, it was during an in climate weather change and his body could not be transported until the weather broke, so he was placed on a first aide stretcher and placed in the freezer in a warehouse until a plane was able to be sent to pick his body up. A body bag was brought when the C-130 plane came into pick his body up. After that we started receiving a supply of body bags. I suppose they wanted us to have plenty on hand.

We had a little shack placed several hundred yards away from base camp that was provided in case of an emergency evacuation. It consisted of an oil stove, survival gear, and a supply of "C" rations and would accommodate personnel until a plane could arrive. Such thing happened on November 16, 1953 when a transmitter building caught fire and in 1963 when a fire broke out in the chow hall, both times shutting down the facility.[2] Depending on the weather at the time required a long wait.

Ground accidents occurred rarely, one of the many duties of steam plant operators was to check on our water supply and pump water as weather permitted to keep the site with plenty of water which we had four 200,000 gallon tanks of which 200,000 gallons was reserved for fire control. These tanks were located on the west side of the site near the Radom and had a ten-degree crown leading from center to the parameter of the tank and the height was fifty feet above the ground. On one such occasion in January I went to the top of one of the tanks to open a hatch to inspect the level. Having snowed the night before, I lost my footing and slid toward the outside edge on my back in the dark (23 hours of darkness this time of year); grabbing for the lowest handrail I managed to stop. If I had not caught myself I would have been another causality of Cape Lisburne and would have required a body bag for me.

Vehicles required engine block heaters here in Alaska. They were installed in all of our vehicles. When they were not being driven they required being plugged into an electrical outlet usually inside the motor pool. When they were being driven the engines had to be kept idling when stopped. On one occasion an airmen turned the vehicle off to go into a building and the oil froze and the engine wouldn't start, it required a salamander heater (Big kerosene heater) to get enough heat to warm the oil to get it started again.

One airman got a little inebriated one night went out on the back stoop of the NCO Club and grabbed a handrail and his hand was frozen to the metal rail. So another airman urinated on his hand in order to get his hand unstuck with out leaving too much skin to the rail. This method was taught in survival school.

Equipment failure was a common thing because of the environment in which it had to operate in. In March of 1970, I noticed that the makeup water pumps were starting to run more often and I monitored the boiler makeup water for a day and it's usage was increasing. I started hunting the source of the leak. I crawled thru all of the maintenance tunnels inspecting pipes and old rusty valves. This took a complete day, having old plans to go by when the facility was built was not an easy task. I then discovered an exposed pipe trough that ran above ground out near where our water gallery was located and ran perpendicular to the runway up toward the engineering building and parallel to the access road to top camp. The plywood lids must have blown off along with the insulation during the storm we had just experienced a few nights before. We experienced 100 mph winds and it dropped to a -135 degrees F that night. It took a crew of three men two months to repair this massive leak, because the weather stayed so cold and we had to endure the snowstorms. I had never seen pipe split at the seams before and this had occurred for several hundred feet. It took us a day to scrounge enough pipes to repair these leaks. The pipe size was two-inch diameter and there was not enough of it, so we improvised by using three-inch diameter pipe with reducers and increasers to make up what pipe of that size we did not have. We had to especially be careful to wear heavy gloves to keep our hands from freezing to the pipe. During this time the boilers were making up feed water at a high rate, so the commander ordered no baths to be taken except once a week, and it had to be an Arctic shower, and absolutely no shaving because we had to maintain 200,000 Gallons for fire protection. The job was finally finished by the first of May.

During another time, at top camp there was another equipment failure but this one was caused by ignorance. There was a five thousand gallon water tank outside of their facilities for their use. There were four recirculating pumps to keep the water recirculating this water to keep it from freezing. The switch to these pumps was a standard light switch mounted next to the light switch for the room. One evening an airman upon examining the site glass to see how much water was left in the tank upon exiting the room turned off the switch to the pumps instead of the lights. I was called to come up and try to fix the situation. I saw the prettiest plume of frozen water cascading off the backside of the mountain into caribou valley you ever did see. We repaired the drain valve, but the tank had to be repaired by engineering out of Elmendorf. A few weeks later when spring arrived the tank was refilled. During this outage the men from top camp were transported to base camp for showers and to do their laundry.

The boiler operators were responsible to keep the drinking water purified by testing the amount of chlorine content and adjusting it accordingly. We had a short culvert turn vertically with concrete poured in the bottom when it was made; in which we added chlorine. There was a small pump that administered the chlorine in parts per million injected into the main water supply. This pump failed and we had to make repairs to it, upon putting it back in service the adjustments were not set to the previous adjustments. So for a day the site personnel experienced a little dysentery. The site medic noticed this because he had to hand out what medicine he had a supply of, but the situation was eventually solved. Everything came out beautifully.

Weather played the biggest factor in surviving at Cape Lisburne, temps would be well

below subfreezing during the winter. On Christmas Eve of 1969 the mail had arrived and letters and packages needed to be transported to top camp and since the road was closed the tram was the only means of transportation to top camp. My roommate at the time (he rotated out before me) was SSGT Schmidt who was the tram operator. On Christmas Eve the weather was very blustery and temps in the subzero range and snowing hard. SSgt Schmidt made the trip up to the landing at top camp, but the wind was holding the tramcar out and away from the landing deck. He had experience with this because he had been transferred to Lisburne from North East Cape on St. Lawrence Island when it was closed in early 1969. Anyway, he had a grappling hook mounted to a pole that he used to grab the rail on the railing of the deck and then he secured the tramcar by tying it off to the deck. He called me on our intercoms phone letting me know that he was not coming back until the next day to give the winds a chance to die down. He spent Christmas with them and returned the following day after Christmas. The tram played a crucial part in the mission at Cape Lisburne.

In June 1970 construction haven been completed the following month and with the old buildings abandoned and removed we moved into the newly composite building. The new boilers were started before the previous three Kewanee's had been taken out of service and replaced by brand new Clever Brooks. We still had three boilers, the engineering captain asked me to work with the Clever Brook representative that was on site to set them up. We went thru the shake down process checking the safety valves, pressure gauges, and general startup procedures. You see we always maintained two boilers on line at a time with one off for standby. It took about eight hours to bring a boiler up to pressure before you could place it on line and then we would take one of the others off line for maintenance. It was always a necessity to keep logs of boiler readings, which was a requirement; we used these readings to calculate heat enthalpy (losses and gains) and efficiency of the boiler. Our two diesel tanks only contained a total of 440,000 gallons of which we shared with the electrical generators. This capacity was all we had for the year until the fuel barge came the next year.

One Friday night in early spring I remember the cooks announced there would be no evening meal served in the chow hall and every one was to meet in the NCO Club. They were cooking Caribou steaks; one of the "White Alice crew" had shot one on a hunting party. Several men hung the carcass up by one of the chain hoist in the motor pool's maintenance building and dressed it out. The meal was served with vegetables and side dishes along with Beer served or Coke for the non-drinkers. I have eaten bear meat before and can be very tough depending on the age of the bear. My Uncle had killed one near his farm in the Great Smoky Mountains here in east Tennessee. The caribou steaks turned out to better than any beefsteaks I had ever eaten even Venison (deer meat).

We had four very fine cooks at Liz. Their morning started at 0400 and ended after the evening meal. Usually three during the day and the other one prepared the midnight chow for the shift workers. As I mentioned previously that we had the finest baker in Alaska, so he started his day around 20:00 baking through the night until around 0600. The Air Force culinary division prepared meals in advance usually two years ahead. To explain this we had the same meals for Monday as we did for the following Monday. This became monotonous for me, so I began missing meals by picking and choosing what I wanted to eat thus this is how I lost sixty-five pounds and my pants had to be taken in. The pants were sewed by yourself because we had no tailor and if that couldn't be accomplished, then you bought fatigue paints through the Post Exchange, which an order had to be placed coming from the main Post Exchange in Elmendorf. Uniforms had to conform to your body.

The chow hall was a place in addition to eating became a social gathering place for those off duty where by airmen drank coffee, chatted, wrote letters home, read books. Some introverts remained in their rooms and read and wrote letters.

All shared barracks duty. Individuals took care of their rooms respectively. Everyone in that hallway sharing and working together did the halls. This was done at least once a week. If the commander did any inspections I wasn't aware of it. We also pitched in and cleaned the showers. This practice carried into the new composite building and its quarters, which were very nice compared to the old wooden quarters that were build in the early 1950's. These new quarters were the state of the art and cost 6.5 million dollars to complete. No one had to go outside in in climate weather except essential personnel.

The new maintenance equipment was even state of the art. We had commodes that would automatically flush when one would rise off of them. This later proved to use too much precious water because we had a limited supply. That feature had to be disabled and returned to manual flushing. Showerheads had a flow rate of five gallons per minute, which as well had to have restrictors. The restrictors limited that rate to two gallons per minute. This reverted to an Arctic shower or some would say a sailor shower. This type of shower one was to wet themselves, soap up, and then rinse. The heating plant was even state of the art. We had three new Clever Brook boilers and not the old worn out Kewanee boilers. These boilers were controlled by a new control panel that monitored the pressures and make up water constantly and a map screen that engineering had made schematic's of the sites piping system with electrical readouts that gave data as to what was functioning and what was not. I no longer had to climb on water tanks to take manual readings. However I still had to go to check on the water at the water gallery and run pumps that delivered water to top camp. Mostly the newer technology was confined to just the composite building itself.

The upper floors of the composite building were restricted to Radar operations and monitoring the top camp Radom data. Electrical key coded locks controlled some of these room's doors. These particular rooms required top-secret clearances to gain entry and were controlled by the communication officer or his designee. Above these floors a conning tower was built for observation.

On the main floor was a sky lighted vestibule that emitted natural light (when available). Around the parameter of this room were the men's quarters. Right off of the vestibule was a movie theatre with state of the art projectors. Modern cushioned theater seating rather than the old chairs. As you came in the front main doors were administrative offices and a cafeteria-style chow hall with all of the newest cooking equipment. It truly was a vast improvement over the older facilities. The newer men that arrived after the first of July 1970 had not known or experienced what we had just given up. I had just spent the last nine months in basic and crude quarters. In the living quarters there were still assigned two men to a room for the enlisted and one man to a room for officers.

The second floor housed a complete library of the newest books as well as older ones with nice comfortable chairs to sit in and the floors were carpeted rather than like the old linoleum floors. The existing pool tables had been moved to this floor as well, but were confined to another part of the room designated as a recreation area.

Life went on getting acquainted with these newer facilities and shake down of all of the new equipment and it's functions. It was summer by now, and we had complete twenty-four hours of daylight, which made for getting to sleep in the evening difficult. This is one of the reasons why the military adapted the twenty-four hour clock. We had black out shades in each room to block the sunlight out. The only difference that I noticed between noon and midnight was the color spectrum of the sun ex: midnight casted an orange hew rather than the traditional yellow that noon produced. Total sunlight is from mid June until late August in this region of the Arctic. The temperatures reached a +72 degree above zero during the day and fell into the low 40's during the evening hours. Believe it or not but in the early spring the temps rose to 0 degrees and I actually sweated in my clothes. I eventually acclimated to the warmer temps.

Summer came along with its insects, which were mosquitoes big enough to fit in the palm of your hand and bit the fool out of you. The state of Texas claimed everything was bigger in Texas, but Alaska had its mosquitoes beat. There were gnats and fly's and you wonder how they survive this far north.

By August it was starting to get closer for my tour of duty to end, so I was packing up personal things that I could not carry on the plane. I was allowed 400 pounds whole baggage because I had gone over my four years enlistment time in July.

These boxes left the site in mid August and I would meet up with them when I returned home. I only kept what necessities I would require for my remaining time on site.

Going back to July, I had been the only heating man from April until then and so I became the NCOIC (non commissioned officer in charge) when an (E3) A/2c arrived. The engineering captain and I had worked together for a while. Also a civilian GS-5 arrived and thought that he outranked me so we had some issues. I really did not care knowing that I only had a few months left. I tried to do my job and keep out of his way. He was tinkering into areas of maintenance that was antiquated. This new system could practically run itself.

The Air Force had started a year before in giving early outs in which I was almost eligible in Dover AFB Delaware, but since I had more than nine months to go I had to take this assignment to Alaska. I had volunteered to go to Vietnam six months earlier (because everyone in my shop at Dover was being sent there so I figured it would be a matter of time before I received orders for Nam) but was not sent because my AFSC (Air Force Service Code) was needed in Alaska. I was within two months of departing Lisburne; the commander was giving some early releases from the site only because they were career men. I approached him but he denied my request. The orderly asked him why and he said, "Wayland is getting out so he can just wait until his year is up". He was mad because he tried his best to get me to reenlist and that would have made him very happy.

As I mentioned earlier that I had lost so much weight (see cover picture) that I was able to take in my fatigue trousers myself, but no way could I alter a class "A" uniform. Our new PX in the composite building carried more items. So, I was able to buy a new class "A" uniform just so I could be mustered out. Seemed like a waste of money to me, but it was a must. I saved money for two months in order to make the purchase.

Now, let me explain why I had to save the money. I only made $80.00/month and my wife drew $100/month for housing allowance, which she received in the mail at home. Every since I had arrived on site and the payroll officer paid us I cashed the check and sent all of the $80.00/month except $5.00/month home in a money order. My wife received her check at home.

My wife stayed with her parents the whole year and although they would not expect a penny from her for her expenses she helped them out and what was left was for her use. We had no children then so there was no baby to feed.

My late Father in law was a WWII veteran having served from D Day all the way to Germany with General Patton. A little know fact, he was General Patton's jeep driver in some areas of that theater. When my wife and I were married he advised us to wait until I got out of service to have children, because he had a son when he was called in service and my wife's sister was born while he was overseas and did not get to see her for fourteen months while he was fighting in WWII. This was good advice.

By the first of September it was getting closer to my DEROS date to leave Cape Lisburne. There was a tradition or rather it was started as a tradition that when you were within ten days you could begin to blow your Cracker Jack whistle. The theater always popped popcorn or sold cracker jacks (remember them) during the movies. You always had a prize in the cracker jacks a toy of some kind, one of the toys were these little colorful whistles. So, you tried to collect yours during the year, when you got one you saved it for such an occasion. These whistles were irritating to the newer troops because you were going home and they were not. Kind of a physiological thing, works on your mind. Unless you have experienced remote isolation one can't understand. Imagine not having seen your wife or husband for a year and suddenly you are going home. Minds can play a lot of dirty tricks on ones inward self. My wife became an inanimate object in my brain. Don't get me wrong I loved her to pieces (we have been happily married now for fifty years), but she had become just a voice on the phone or words on paper. As the date gets closer you get excited to leave.

The evening before I left and haven packed my duffle bag. I went around saying good by to my closest friends, took in a movie, showered and retired for the night. I rose at 0500 and went to breakfast. The fire chief SSgt. Parkhurst was leaving also along with an airman that got a Dear John letter and was granted emergency leave to go home to try and patch his marriage. After Breakfast we gathered where our belongings were sitting at the loading dock to be taken by us to the airstrip. Operations announced over the speaker system that Wein airlines was a half hour out. Our old friend Pelch was piloting the plane. This was Thursday September 17, 1970. And the weather was sunny but snow was on the ground from a few days before when it had begun to snow again. The temp was dropping and winter was just about on us again. So we were all anxious to get on board and leave.

A little after 0900 we airlifted from the runway going in a NNE direction, Pelch made a wide sweep over the Chukchi Sea one last time so we could see Liz for the last time. We headed South East for Kotzebue, which was 164 miles away. I remember we had all of the seats attached to the floor unlike when I first arrived and filled in that little twin otter plane. Some of the other passenger's, I can't remember who they all were, maybe have been some construction workers rotating out. There were whoops and hollers from the military guys except the troop that received his Dear John letter for he had to return in ten days. There was some chatter but some of us were mostly quite.

SSgt Parkhurst and I were going to be staying in the transit barracks at Elmendorf for a night. He was career and was on his last enlistment going home to his family in Charleston SC the next day after we turned in our cold weather gear and a debriefing. I wasn't leaving Alaska until the following Monday for McCord AFB in Seattle, Wash. I also had to take a medical physical at Ft. Richardson, Alaska located 35 miles from Elmendorf.

The plane reached Kotzebue and we deplaned. We had an hour to wait until the big DC-9 of the Alaskan Airlines arrived to take us to Anchorage by way of Fairbanks. This was around 10:00am. We boarded the DC-9 picked our seats and immediately noticed the women stewardess you can't imagine what a sight that was to behold. It had been one year since we had seen a beautiful female or a matter of fact any female. She was used to this reacquainting welcoming of airmen to society.

We landed at Fairbanks to refuel and to let us stretch our legs and were told it would be about an hour before the plane took off. It was now high noon. Some of us went into the air terminal for coffee and doughnuts. We were to be served a meal on our flight back to Anchorage. Around 1300 we lifted off to an altitude of ~30,000 feet for Anchorage. We were above the weather and the tops of clouds were like a pillow.

Around 1600 we were approaching Anchorage and were told to fasten seat belts that we would be landing at Anchorage International Airport and not Elmendorf. We gathered our belongings and said our good bye's to the airmen on emergency leave and wished him well. He was to catch the next plane to the lower Forty-eight. SSgt Parkhurst and I boarded an Air Force Bus to be taken to Elmendorf. Upon going through the security gates we proceeded to the transit barracks where the bus driver let us out. The scene was very familiar to us because just a year before we had stayed in this very barracks. Seemed like home but a home you did not want to stay long in.

After checking in with ops we were assigned our room. SSgt Parkhurst and I arranged to be in the same quad across from each other. By this time it was 1800 so we went to chow in the nice chow hall at the transit barracks.

The following morning, a Friday, SSgt Parkhurst and I went together to the clothing warehouse to turn our Parkas and cold weather gear in and we parted company for the remainder of the day but was to meet back up in the evening at the transit barracks. After getting my affairs done, I boarded a bus to be taken to Ft. Richardson for my mustering out medical. The bus ride took me about an hour because Ft. Richardson is located in the mountains thirty-five miles away. The physical took all the rest of the day and I ate lunch while there. As I was going through the routine I was waiting outside of x-ray and they wheeled a troop out that had just come from surgery. It appeared he had a steel plate inserted into his cranium and was still out of it. The nurse informed me that he had been medevac'd out of Vietnam just the day before. I saw some pretty gruesome injuries there. The doctor was my last stop, he examined me from head to toe, I have never had so a through physical in my life. He asked if I had any problems physiological problems. I told him I had none. It was a beautiful fall afternoon just like back home in Tennessee and the bus ride was very enjoyable back to Elmendorf.

I met up with SSgt Parhurst and had our last meal together before retiring for the night. He was all set for the *Freedom Bird* the next morning to McCord and on to Charleston S.C. He left sometime during the early morning hours before the sun rose.

The first thing I wanted to get that Saturday morning was to get a real haircut and send a telegram home telling my wife that I had arrived and was to arrive in Seattle on Monday. I went to the PX to purchase some mementos and returned to the barracks. In doing so I took in the view of Mt. McKinley, which the view was crystal clear, and you could see the top peak. It's hard to explain how that you had to throw your head way back to see the crest of the mountain because it was so high. It was all covered with snow and was just magnificent and spectacular. This reminded me of Mt. Le Conte back home in the Smokey's were I had made a many of a trip as a kid.

That afternoon after taking in a movie and returning to the barracks I ran into my old NCOIC from Dover AFB (the one I had two years previously) and he was a M/Sgt. We renewed acquaintances' and chatted a while. He invited me to his quarters and we continued our conversations. After chow I returned to my quad to get some rest.

Along about 2200 a group of Army soldiers came in to occupy the rest of the quad. I asked where they were headed since they were traveling as a unit. One of them told me a place in Vietnam (long forgotten the name of the place). During the night I heard movement but didn't awake to investigate, just assumed it was those Army troops moving out. It was, as I discovered in the morning and they had left a solider behind. They did not bother to wake him as I found out later, so he was AWOL (absent without leave) and was in serious trouble. When he went down to the barracks control center and inquired as to where his unit was they informed him his company had left five hours ago so the MP's were called. The M.Sgts. from Dover and I inquired as to what was going on and could we be of assistance. The MP's arrived as we were all standing around and I told them what I had heard and the M.Sgt. was down stairs as the soldier's unit left and overheard one of them say "just leave him up there". We both signed affidavits to these facts. The authorities made arrangements to put him on a plane to Vietnam. Given the facts and our sworn statement he was not charged with AWOL. I attended church services and read a book the rest of Sunday.

The M.Sgt. had warned me to be on time early Monday morning Sept. 21st because it was first come first served to get on the military manifest. He was career and had spent a lot of time traveling in the military. I took his advice and called a base taxi at 0400 Monday morning to take me to the terminal. I boarded a C-141 going to McCord AFB in Tacoma, Wash. We arrived about 1400 and had to go through customs before seeking quarters. After settling in, I inquired as to what chow hall was the best to go to. I boarded the base bus and went to chow. After chow I found a pay phone (remember those? they stood on corners that you could throw quarters in) and called my wife, we spent some time on the phone and I informed her I would call her in route home and it could be sometime early Wednesday. The bus driver informed me at McCord that I needed to be at this certain building by 0700 and if I were late I could not get processed out until the following day, which would be the 23rd of September.

So, as you might guess (really now!!) I was anxious to get out and be home. I left the transit barracks after showering and shaving to be at this building by 0700. At 0500 I was waiting on the steps of the building. An officer walking by told me they didn't open until 0800 and it would be a long wait. I informed him that I didn't mind and he struck up a short conversation with me asking if I were stationed there and I told him I had come from a remote radar station at the top of the world. He asked which one so I told him Cape Lisburne and he was not familiar with that one but had been stationed at Anchorage before. If you have never served at one of these locations people just make idle conversation, because they don't seem to care. I bided him farewell and he wished me luck so, I saluting his rank and he went on his merry way. After a while someone came along to open the doors and I formed a line by being the first in line.

The first Air Force personnel person looked at my orders and saw where I was to be discharge for "convenience of the government" relieving me of active duty. He asked why I was getting out, he just did not get it and looked at some other paper work he had and told me if I would just reenlist I would have my SSgt stripes. He had those promotion orders in his hands. I was shocked! Remember I mentioned that the commander was mad because I would not reenlist? Well, he had held my promotion over my head and I was furious that he stooped so low to bury the paper work. Since I did not reenlist the promotion was a mute issue.

Listening to different guest from different agencies and being informed of our rights and opportunities offered veterans we were through when the paper work was signed. We were informed since by this time it was near noon, that payroll had gone to lunch and we would have to go there to get paid. In the mean time we were asked how many of us did they want to procure air transportation for. So, a JAMTO (Joint Air Military Transport Organization) representative took our names and made the necessary arrangements. I hesitated at first because this same organization made arrangements for me years before when I left basic training at Amarillo, TX and it took a week flying military standby including waiting hours and days in airport terminals to get home to my hometown.

Since it was lunchtime several of us decided to go to the NCO club and get some lunch and go to payroll office afterwards after which we would procure transport to Tacoma, Seattle airport. Three others and I shared the cost of the cab for the thirty-five mile ride to Seattle. The cab fare was Thirty-five dollars. This was quite a sum of money in those days, which equated to a dollar a mile. After looking at the time we were sure we would not make the 2:00pm flight going east. Some of the party was going south to Austin, TX and some were going to California. One of the fares tried to get the cab driver to speed up and he informed him that no amount of money could entice him to speed. The police fine for speeding in the Seattle area was a hefty one. We eventually arrived at the airport and after checking in and being assured we had a seat (we were flying military stand-by) and would not be bumped we went to the concourse where the flight was and waited for the boarding. This plane was gigantic and nothing like I had seen before but read about the year before when it was in production. This plane was a 747 that had originated its flight in Tokyo Japan and its final destination was New York City. We were informed that the delay was because they did not have enough passengers which required three hundred people minimum.

After they reached the required minimum of passengers we boarded the aircraft. Inside was just gorgeously decked out with all of the amenities. We even had a movie screen in the compartment we were in. There was a beautiful stair case that took you aloft to a mezzanine in the front of the plane which consisted of a bar and lounge.

Around five in the evening we were cleared for take off and taxied to the active runway. As the pilot was given the go ahead the plane roared down the runway with it's four powerful engines at full throttle and we lifted off and climbed at a forty-five degree angle and you were literally plastered to the back of your seat. When the plane reached forty thousand feet we leveled off and were headed east for a stop in Chicago, Ill where I was to change to a smaller plane and go south to Cincinnati, Ohio and on to my hometown.

After we reached our altitude we asked the stewardess if we could watch a movie, her response was they would not have enough time to show it because the plane over the continental Unites States would be too short and they had just showed a movie over the Pacific. This was unbelievable, so I asked what the speed was and she informed me that we were going eight hundred miles an hour. The plane made noise and creaked as the airframe moved through the sky. Shortly I felt as though we were circling and we were. The pilot announced that he was circling over Minneapolis, Min in a holding pattern until the air traffic cleared at O'Hara airport in Chicago and then we would land soon. He told us he would notify us as to when to put our seat belts on. It was approximately 2230 and we were served refreshments and we continued to circle until he announced that we were going into Chicago.

It was dark by now as we landed and deplaned. I immediately went to the luggage area to claim my luggage and walk to another smaller plane that would take me home. This plane was a DC-9 operated by Delta airlines just like I had left Kotzebue on and it seemed so small compared to the big 747 operated by Northwest Orient airlines coming from Tokyo. The ticket clerk informed us that there would be an hour delay, so I made a phone call to my wife, she had been up all night waiting to pick me up at the airport in Knoxville. I informed her that I should be landing in Knoxville by 0400. After hanging up I bought myself a cup of coffee and tried to relax, but the excitement of seeing her again after twelve months was just too over whelming.

We boarded and took off with one brief stop in Cincinnati, Ohio to pick up some passengers going to Florida and we were air borne again. In was a beautiful starry night sky lit by a full moon. Off in the distance I saw this cluster of light from the window in which I was seated. The stewardess's had turned off the cabin lights since it was a red eye flight so people could sleep. I knew those lights were my hometown and I would soon be home. The excitement grew as we approached Knoxville and as we were preparing to land, I briefly reflected on the last four years in the military and how much the world had changed in just a year and would my wife have changed and how much I had changed and would things be the same. I knew I had changed, the solitude in which I had just experienced made me appreciate life much more and how materialistic things didn't mean much and how I did not talk as much as I had before I left and I moved at a slower pace.

I was suddenly jolted back to reality and brought back from my thoughts on these things in my mind, as we were approaching the runway with wheels down and about to have the rubber meet the ground again.

As I deplaned and walked down the portable steps to the ground and toward the fence, this time of the morning everything was very quite in the airport except for the cleaning crew and a few people waiting on loved ones or friends, As I had been traveling in a full dress blue uniform of the United States Air Force with all of my ribbons displayed I saw my wife standing there and I rushed into her loving arms and I sure was glad to be home. Her late brother Edward Webb and her late Mother had brought her to the airport to meet me. She would have come alone but her brother advised against it being so late in the night.

The next day was a beautiful fall day absent of the subzero temps I had experienced all year and the trees were beginning to turn to paint beautiful colors in East Tennessee. I had missed so much of little things that I had taken for granted before going to Alaska. I was craving these little small hamburgers called "Krystal's" in some parts of the Country in the south they are called "White castle burgers". These little burgers are about three Inches Square and covered containing onions and mustard and a pickle. So, we drove to one of these Krystal Hamburger stands near the apartment that my wife had rented for us two months prior to my return home. Between the two of us we ate two dozen of these gut burgers. I only weighed one hundred and sixty five pounds and I wasn't worried about gaining the weight.

The days were Happy and wonderful days that followed getting acquainted with society and in traveling around my driving were too slow for my wife's liking because I was in a fast pace world now. My wife would reach over with her foot and place it on top of mine in order for us to speed up. I wasn't used to this speed because ten miles an hour was top speed driving the few roads we had at Cape Lisburne.

I had been paid eight hundred dollars muster out pay and with a one hundred dollar a month apartment I had to find a job, but since I had accumulated thirty days leave and paid for it from the service I could not be gainful employed in civilian life until the thirty days were up. After thirty days passed I went back to the company I had worked for when I was called in to service, and was told by the Military upon discharge they had to give me my old job back but only had to keep me for thirty days tops. So, I did, and they were not thrilled at all and they would have to find a place for me. I told the new supervisor that under those circumstances I would rather find a secure job that I could rely on. I left with hard feelings, but so much time had passed since I worked for them that it didn't matter because I was looking for a job when I went to work for them seven years prior.

We were called "Baby Killers" since we had served our country during the Vietnam conflict years and were looked down upon. Some by stander, maybe a draft dodger who knows, spit upon me once in the Seattle airport. Then I come home to a job that no longer was there for me. Oh Well, I must move on, so after pounding the streets during the later month of November I came to realize that hunting a job was not so easy. The job world had changes so much in the years I had been absent from. Now you had to go through a personnel manager before you could be interviewed. I also had competition with other solders coming back from the war. I had been a draftsman before entering the service and I really didn't want to pursue that occupation again. I was a hand's on guy and used to working with tools but there just were no jobs for that trade available except for guys that their companies were nice enough to take them back.

In late November and the finances running low I was forced to pursue my previous occupation as a draftsman. So, having been to Employment firms (Head Hunters) and walking the streets searching for a job, at the end of the day I was about to return home I came upon a company that looked like it might hire. I stopped in and asked the receptionist if they had any jobs needed in the engineering field. She told me as a matter of fact that a Mr. Johnson the chief engineer needed someone. She asked if I could wait until she checked with him. She came back and told me he wanted to talk to me. I told him I had just been released from active duty and was hunting a job. It was late, and they closed at 5:00pm. He asked if I could draw something. So, I gave him a sample of my work and he told me he would get back with me.

I was called to be interviewed by the personnel manager on a Friday and was hired Saturday and reported to work on Monday December 2 1970.

I worked for them for eighteen months until they voted to bring a union in and I later obtained a job at the Tennessee Valley Authority, a government agency, and studied and went to school and became an Engineering Aide. I stayed with them for thirteen years until they wanted to re assign me permanently to Browns Ferry nuclear steam plant in Athens, Ala.
Later, I worked for Oak Ridge National Laboratory for eighteen years as an engineer doing piping design. I retired from there in 2003 and spend time with my family now. I have a daughter who is forty-six and a Granddaughter who is Nineteen. She attends College. She just finished her freshman year.

Dedication of My Adventure To:

Until Leslie Randal found my video on YouTube and I finding another retired airmen M.Sgt. Gary Johnson (RET.) who made a career out of the Air Force and was stationed at the Cape when her grandparents lost their lives July 16, 1966. I had not really thought about the Cape except for snippets of my memory. This has been an adventure over these past several months in trying to remember this place. This prompted me to write this for posterity so it could be past down in my family and tell others of my long ago adventures that I endured in the arctic at the top of the world. As the lyric's say in the Disney song "It's a small world after all". More pictures can be found at www.youtube.com search for *The Land of the Midnight Sun 1969-1970*. Turn the sound up and enjoy.

Pictures

Winter road to Top Camp   Back Side of Cape Lisburne-frozen Sea

Airstrip in winter next to Chukchi Sea   White Alice

Explanation of Pictures from top to bottom: Winter road to top camp when open, otherwise the tramcar was used. Back side of the new facilities at Cape Lisburne 1970. The Chukchi Sea can be seen in the background and notice it is frozen. This is the airstrip in the winter after it had been cleared expecting a flight due to land soon. In total darkness firepots were lit and placed on both sides of the runway. This part of the White Alice station.

Caribou at top camp

Point Hope Eskimo Village

Twin Otter plane lifting off airstrip

Twenty Third hour of Darkness [4]

Explanation of Pictures from top to bottom Caribou wondered from caribou valley below to top camp. They don't seem to fear man, Point Hope approx. twenty-five miles south of camp another Eskimo Village and on the Bering sea, Twin Otter operated by Wein airline company brought supplies and had the mail contract, In the land of the midnight sun, darkness which occurs between late October until late February which only gave us darkness for twenty three hours in a day, The other hour of the day is twilight time, and this picture shows that time of the day.

---

[4] Picture from Alaskan historical museum

Midnight Sun

Looking from Tramcar North

Mt. McKinley in Distance

Wein Twin Otter aircraft on tarmac

Explanation of pictures: Midnight sun occurred from late May through late August and started on the horizon and rotated in a circular pattern and revolved in a 360-degree circle in twenty-four hours. This progression continued as the sun rose spherically until it reached straight up. Looking from tramcar north was taken on my first trip to top camp; Mt. McKinley was taken from the window of the plane on the way to Anchorage. Wein Twin Otter aircraft on tarmac was taken at Cape Lisburne when we were about to have a White Out.

Track master circa 1966 (Gary Johnson)   711 AC&W HQ at Cape Lisburne[5]

Muir Birds nest circa 1966

---

[3] Pictures taken by M.Sgt. Gary Johnson 1966 by permission

This is the official document proving that I served above the Arctic Circle and a member of the Arctic Circle Club and a lifetime member. Presented to me, as I was departing the Cape by Maj. Gordon E Kirkpatrick new commander of the 711th AC&W Squadron at Cape Lisburne, AK in 1970 and also MSGT Harry S. Brown First Sergeant.

Concluding Information on the demise of the Cold War and dismantling of the DEW-Line Stations

Cape Lisburne (Liz1) was closed on November 1, 1983 among other Cold War sites along the DEWLine due to budget cuts in operating cost of these top cover stations and replaced with digital satellite stations reporting their data to Elmendorf AFB located in Anchorage Alaska. The

Secretary of the Air Force in 1969 deemed these sites too expensive to operate and ordered plans for closing them. One of such sites was North East Cape on St. Lawrence Island (Located in the Bering Sea Half way to Russia), which was very expensive to operate, and was closed in September 1969.

After the closures and Airman were transferred to other assignments across the globe and these cold war radar sites sat idle and abandoned for decades and became in dereliction and ruins. Most of the Antenna's and Radar equipment were removed from these sites in the 80's. To date twenty-one of these sites have been abandoned across the DEWLine and Canada.

Now comes the clean up in the mid to late 1990's. Concerns are to how to dispose of all the PCB's from the oil storage tanks and other equipment and paint on these sites. It won't be easy and will be very expensive. The environment is supposed to be restored to its original pre DEWLine conditions. This will be no small undertaking for an area that has been a military site for more than forty decades. The cleanup is now underway to restore the land back to pre-1950 status,

Cape Lisburne now sits with just a small building to house the generators and allow short-term civilian personal to check on its equipment several times a month using the old existing runway for landings. Along with a Satellite dish aimed at the heavens that are all that's left of the site. The new composite building that was built between 1969 and 1970 at a cost of 6.5 million dollars was demolished.

It was an adventure that I was privileged to have served and one in my memories that I'll never forget.

Technology and policy have reshaped the sites of electronic packages enabling radar operations and camps that initially housed hundreds of military personnel now house tiny crews of private contractors and operated by ARCTEC (main offices are in Anchorage Alaska). Technicians make between $120,000-$150,000/per years salary's with remote time cut to only a few months at a time as opposed to extended stays of one year away from civilization. In my day we didn't have that privilege because of the distance, isolation, and the commitment of a one-year tour with no leave.

As I mentioned before that in 1969 some general in Washington DC deemed these old sites too expensive to maintain and operate. In 2017 ARCTEC was awarded a 37.9 million dollar contract for maintain and operating these new LRR sites with satellite technology and minimal crews.

As the world changes and since the late General Hap Arnold deemed that Alaska and the Northern Arctic was a valued area. He said that anyone could go any where in the world within twelve hours venturing the Arctic air route. That's why we must remain diligent of this region to monitor the skies for anything that's not supposed to be there particular long-range bombers from Russia.

Today the older TU-95 Bears aircraft are flying sorties and tontine country's all across many places in the world. The world is a restless place and we must maintain our freedom, as we know it.

As one of many DEW-Liners I wanted to give an audience an insight as to what life was like and the adventure that I had the privilege to experience in just a long-short of the year or years that a DEW-Liner endures to keep these sites operational. Some times it takes a village to maintain the surveillance of our enemies. ***PRO PATRIA VIGILANTES**

Reunion's

In April of 2018, I saw an up coming reunion for anyone that ever served on a Radar station in the world on www.togetherweserved.com of which I am a member. The fifteenth reunion of the 664th AC&W squadron in Bellefontaine, Ohio was scheduled for June 22-24, 2018.

I asked my daughter if she would like to go with me and she agreed. I made the reservations and the hotel accommodations. On June 22 in the early morning hours we left for the reunion. It's a six-hour trip from where I live.

We had a fantastic time meeting so many wonderful people and their wife's. It was such a joy to share some of our experiences. I wasn't stationed here but, so many shared similar stories and not being a Radicand myself I learned a lot about Radar in Just talking to these people. Thanks to the ones I talked to including Robert Macaluso, and especially Tom Simpson who we shared a base that we had both been stationed on (Orlando Air Force Base) even though he was their five years before me.

I also meet Maya Hirschman curator/manager of *The Secrets of Radar Museum* located in London, ON from her I learned that the English developed the original Radar concept.

If, you were ever in this area of the country I would encourage you to visit this museum. It is located on the highest point in Ohio.

In talking to Bryan Jefferies earlier in the year he told me that typically Radar people rarely have reunions due to the sites having such small numbers in personnel. Bryan was the youngest DEWliner and served at Halls Branch Canada on the DEW line. He resides in Ottawa Canada. He volunteers at "The Diefenbunker, Canada's Cold War Museum" on the web at www.Diefenbunker.ca

References

[1] *Alaskan Air Command History Elmendorf AFB*

[2] *Radar Museum.Com/Cape Lisburne/documents/Commanders Report*

[3] *Pictures are from M.Sgt. Gary Johnson's Tour; circa 1966 collection. By Permission from Gary*

[4] *Alaskan Historical Museum Anchorage, Alaska*

All pictures in this book were taken by Sgt. Wayland, except as noted and the included Artic Circle Certification certificate contributed by Sgt. Wayland.

The Artwork rendering of the mountains of Alaska and the Aura Borealis was made and contributed by my Granddaughter Bonnie Rose.

Rendering made by Bonnie Rose of the Northern Lights known as the *Aura Borealis*

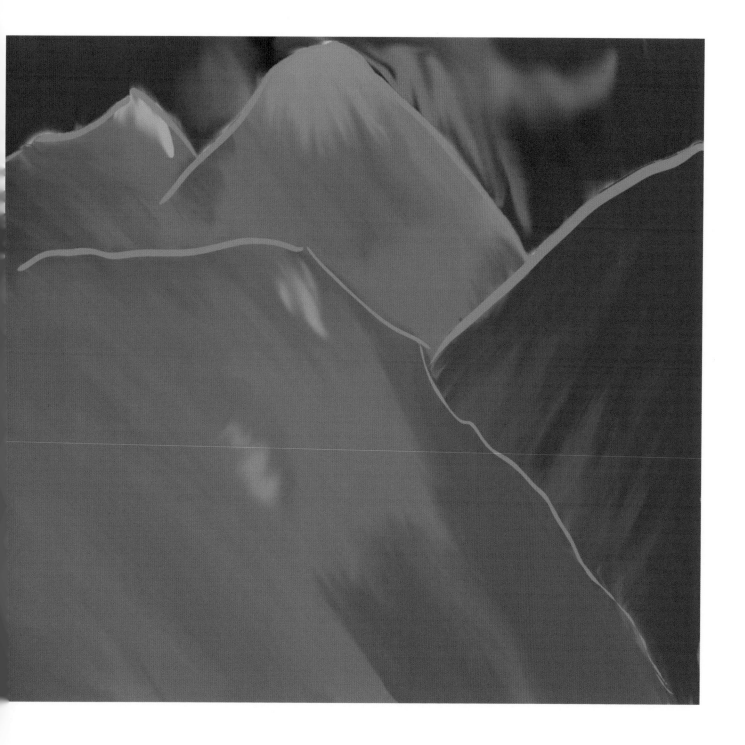

Printed in Great Britain
by Amazon